PHOTOS THAT MADE
U.S. HISTORY

PHOTOS THAT MADE U.S. HISTORY

Volume 1: From the Civil War Era to the Atomic Age

· *Edward Wakin* ·

with Daniel Wakin

WALKER AND COMPANY

NEW YORK

First published in the United States of America in 1993 by Walker Publishing Company, Inc.

Published simultaneously in Canada by Thomas Allen & Son Canada, Limited, Markham, Ontario

Library of Congress Cataloging-in-Publication Data
Wakin, Edward.
Photos that made U.S. history/Edward Wakin with Daniel Wakin.
p.   cm.
Includes index.
Contents: v. 1. From the Civil War era to the atomic age—v. 2. From
the Cold War to the space age.
Summary: Presents photographs (and their stories) that became
almost as famous as the history-making events they depicted.
Includes Lincoln, Nixon and Krushchev, Iwo Jima, Kent State, and
others.
ISBN 0-8027-8230-2 (v. 1).—ISBN 0-8027-8231-0 (lib. bdg. : v.
1).—ISBN 0-8027-8270-1 (v. 2).—ISBN 0-8027-8272-8 (lib. bdg. :
v. 2)
1. United States—History—1865–   —Pictorial works—Juvenile
literature.   2. Photography—United States—History—Juvenile
literature.   [1. United States—History—1865–   2. Photography—
History.]   I. Wakin, Daniel.   II. Title.
E661.W32   1993
973.9′022′2—dc20   93-12096
CIP
AC

Designed by Brandon Kruse
Printed in Mexico

2   4   6   8   10   9   7   5   3   1

Contents

Photographs

Introduction

···

AN IMAGE-BUILDING PHOTOGRAPH of presidential hopeful Abraham Lincoln . . .

A stunning view of what would become the highlight of Yellowstone National Park . . .

A sordid scene in New York slums at the turn of the century . . .

A close-up of a desperate mother and children trapped in the hunger and poverty of the Great Depression . . .

An unforgettable portrait of a heroic flag-raising during World War II . . .

A nightmare image of a mushroom cloud . . .

···

When it comes to making as well as recording history, the camera has demonstrated that it can be mightier than the pen. At crucial moments in U.S. history, the photograph has been both a punctuation point and an animating force.

As punctuation point, a photograph has marked off a major episode, a historic part of our past.

As an animating force, a photograph can influence, shape, and direct public reaction and in this way help to make history.

This book will show history-making photographs and tell the story of how they helped to make history. Each photograph is worth seeing on its own merits and also depicts events important to know in order to understand ourselves as a people and as a nation.

Photography's history-recording and history-making dates from its invention in the 1830s. The photographer has acted as witness, the photograph as evidence. The public has responded as judge and jury, pronouncing sentence by the way it reacted.

By influencing the way Americans vote, act, and join (or don't join) in national efforts, these photos have helped to make U.S. history. Looking at the images in this book means coming face to face with our history while it was being made. The experience expands our understanding of who we are and how we as a nation have reached this point.

Each history-making photograph has four elements, which are intertwined, but also separate.

1. *The Event:* What was happening directly involved Americans, and they were caught up in the situation and the circumstances. What was happening both involved and affected them. They were part of the action.

2. *The Image:* The photographs captured what was happening as only a picture can. They cut through thousands of words, eliminated complications, overrode arguments for and against, pushed aside second thoughts. They made Americans at the time and

Americans today feel what they saw. The images cut to the quick, said it all—almost.

3. *The Effect*: Something happened because of these photographs. Americans changed the way they felt; government leaders were stopped in their tracks; votes, laws, decisions were influenced, even shaped. All of this happened within a historical setting. The context and the circumstances turned the image into a history-maker.

4. *The Photographer*: The hand that held the camera did much more than push the button. The attentive eye, the responsive heart, and the alert mind came into play. These photographs celebrate photography and the men and women who dedicate themselves to enabling us to see the world and to help us grasp it.

In looking—really looking—at these photographs, we gain a double return. First, we come into contact with powerful images, appreciated for their own sake and experienced as part of the visual world that surrounds us. Second, we see U.S. history as something alive.

What is history but a story of what men and women do for themselves and to themselves—through war and peace, campaigns and elections, fads, fashions, and social movements? It's a story of how people live during and through different times in different ways.

But what a story!

Since the middle of the last century, it's been a story accompanied by pictures. Here are some that did more than help tell the story: They helped to make it.

PHOTOS THAT MADE U.S. HISTORY

Abraham Lincoln (February 27, 1860) by Mathew B. Brady.
(Courtesy of the Library of Congress)

· 1 ·

Making Lincoln Look "Impressive"

· · ·

Building the Presidential Image of
Abraham Lincoln

ON FEBRUARY 27, 1860, a tall, awkward man from Illinois walked into the most fashionable photo studio in New York. His legs were much too long for his body. He had a long head, large ears, flabby cheeks, and a big Adam's apple.

At six feet four inches, he towered over an artistic-looking photographer who sported a black, pointed beard and peered at his visitor through wire-rimmed glasses.

The photographer, Mathew B. Brady, was face to face with Abraham Lincoln, whose supporters had launched a Lincoln-for-president campaign. But he didn't yet have the nomination of the new Republican party. He still had to convince voters and political leaders that he was "presidential" in style, appearance, and leadership qualities.

In the photo studio on Broadway at Tenth Street, the photographer and his subject represented two different success stories of nineteenth-century America.

Lincoln, born February 12, 1809, in a Kentucky log cabin,

spent his youth on a frontier farm in Indiana. His father, Thomas, was an outgoing farmer who loved to tell stories. His mother, Nancy, was a sad-eyed woman devoted to the Baptist religion. Abraham inherited his father's love of storytelling and his mother's melancholy.

Neither father nor mother had any education, and all Abraham Lincoln could manage was one year of formal schooling. But he had an ambition: to be "truly esteemed of my fellow men." He educated himself and set about learning the law. After obtaining his attorney's license, he moved to Springfield, Illinois, to practice law and pursue politics.

By the time Lincoln walked into Brady's studio, he had made his mark as a lawyer, as an Illinois state legislator, and as a U.S. congressman. Although he had lost a race for the U.S. Senate in 1858, he won respect for his part in seven momentous debates with Stephen A. Douglas on slavery. As historian Stephen B. Oates points out, Lincoln's views on slavery came down to one basic point: "Slavery was *wrong* and opposition to it was *right*."

The man on the other side of the camera, "Brady of Broadway," was an urban American success story. Brady was born in upstate New York, of poor Irish parents. He arrived penniless in New York at the age of sixteen with an interest in art and painting.

He soon turned to photography and studied an early form of photography, the daguerreotype. This was the fixing of a photographic image on a copper plate with the help of chemicals. Brady's skill was such that he went to London in 1851 and won the top medals for daguerreotype portraits at the Crystal Palace Exhibition.

In New York, Brady opened photo studios that captured the attention of important New Yorkers. He became famous by photographing the famous, and in his studio he created a gallery of the people he photographed. New Yorkers came just to see his latest celebrity portraits. His photographs were the talk of the town.

As photographic technology progressed, Brady began using the wet-plate process, a major improvement over photos on copper plates. By the time Brady opened the gallery visited by Lincoln, he was acclaimed by *The New York Times* as "the prince of photographers on our side of the water."

When Brady saw Lincoln, he wondered how he was going to make him look "impressive," like someone who could lead the nation amid the burning controversy over slavery. When Lincoln arrived for the photo session, both his mood and appearance were problematic.

Brady saw a man who looked "haggard and careworn" and who showed all the signs of "protracted suffering." Lincoln wore a black suit made of broadcloth that was wrinkled and didn't fit him. His tie was no more than a black ribbon, and his shoes obviously hurt his feet.

Lincoln wore a low shirt collar that made his neck look even longer than it was. Brady later recalled that he asked Lincoln whether he could rearrange his collar.

"Ah," said Lincoln, "I see you want to shorten my neck."

Brady answered, "That's just it." They both laughed, and Lincoln relaxed.

There was another problem. Lincoln was too tall for the "immobilizer," the clamp used to hold a sitter's head in place during picture-taking. Brady had to prop it up so it would be high enough.

Knowing he would have "great trouble in making a natural

picture," Brady drew on all his skills as a celebrated portrait pho-tographer and shot away. At the time, he could not know how important his photograph would turn out to be.

While Lincoln posed for Brady, his mind was on the speech he was going to deliver that evening at the Cooper Institute. New York was of major importance to his presidential ambitions. He faced a tough audience of elite New Yorkers coming to hear "the Westerner."

The speech would set forth Lincoln's principles for the voting public. Brady's photograph would show what Lincoln looked like, something that was also important to the voters. There was a widespread feeling at the time that you could tell a great deal about a person by his or her appearance, particularly if the person was a politician. Lincoln's opponents were saying that he didn't look the part of a national leader. They made fun of his looks.

As it turned out, the Cooper Institute speech and the Brady photograph combined to make history. Years later, Brady told a newspaper reporter that Lincoln once said: "Brady and the Cooper Institute made me President."

Lincoln had been nervous about addressing a New York audi-ence when he boarded a train to come east. He worked hard on an antislavery speech. In particular, his research showed that of the thirty-nine men who signed the U.S. Constitution, twenty-one had voted at one time or another to exclude slavery from the national territories being settled in the West. That was the posi-tion he took in his speech: Keep slavery out of the new territories.

When he arrived in New York, a snowstorm was battering the city as 1,500 shivering New Yorkers gathered at the Cooper Insti-tute. They applauded politely as Lincoln mounted the platform.

He then began speaking in his high-pitched voice with its Kentucky twang.

According to the poet Carl Sandburg, who wrote a famous biography of Lincoln: "He was slow getting started. There were Republicans not sure whether to laugh or feel sorry. As he got into his speech there came a change. They saw he thought his way deeply among the issues and angers of the hour."

At one dramatic point in the speech, Lincoln challenged Americans to oppose the spread of slavery: "Let us have faith that right makes right, and in that faith, let us, to the end, dare to do our duty as we understand it."

As he spoke, he was frequently interrupted with cheers and loud applause. When he finished, the audience gave him a standing ovation and waved hats and handkerchiefs. People rushed onto the platform to congratulate him. One reporter wrote: "No man ever before made such an impression on his first appeal to a New York audience."

The speech was a triumph. It was printed and praised in newspapers and reprinted in mass-circulation pamphlets that were read by voters throughout the country. Lincoln won over party leaders in the Northeast, and the speech's impact reached Illinois, convincing even opponents that he was presidential timber. His oratory had shown that.

But there was the matter of how Lincoln looked, particularly at a time when the political photograph was gaining importance. When Lincoln won the Republican nomination, in May 1860, and then campaigned for the presidency, his face became widely known from photographs, particularly popular small photographs called cartes de visite. Magazines ran woodcut engravings showing Lincoln. Currier and Ives reproduced Brady's portrait in lithographs. The 1860 campaign also was marked by the introduction of photographic campaign buttons.

Everywhere, Americans saw Brady's photo of Lincoln, but what stood out was *not* what Brady saw in person. Brady saw a man whose "head was long and tall from the base of the brain to the eyebrow. His ears were large, his nose long and blunt, the tip of it rather ruddy, and slightly awry towards the right-hand side; his chin, projecting far and sharp, curved upward to meet a thick lower lip which hung downward; his cheeks were flabby, and the loose skin fell in wrinkles or folds; there was a large mole on his right cheek and an uncommonly prominent Adam's apple on his throat."

The Brady photograph created a far different impression. As historian and Lincoln biographer Oates states: "The photograph revealed a beardless fifty-one-year-old Lincoln, with a receding hairline, a mole on his right cheek, and a firm and steady gaze in his eyes. He wore a new black broadcloth suit, a vest, a stiff white shirt, and a black tie. With his left hand on a stack of books, he looked like a learned statesman, tall, straight, and sure of himself."

Brady of Broadway had succeeded once again in portraying the famous and the fashionable at their best. He called into play all the tools of his photographic trade: headrest and clamp, backdrop and prop, lighting and retouching. He added his talent for selecting the best angle and position for taking the photograph.

The photo retains its power today, particularly in the intent look on Lincoln's face. His deep-set, dark eyes are penetrating. They give the impression of a man who both thinks and feels at a deep level. Here is a man who must be taken seriously.

Lincoln stands erect, facing the camera at an angle; he looks strong and firm. The left hand resting on the stack of books creates a forceful triangle that both caresses and controls the book on top.

Lincoln's own youthful goal is a fitting caption for the image presented in the Brady photograph: "truly esteemed of my fellow men." It also agrees with the verdict of history for one of the greatest presidents in the history of the United States.

Old Faithful (1871) by William Henry Jackson.
(*Courtesy of the National Park Service*)

· 2 ·

Saving a "Wonderland" for Everyone

*Recording the Wonders
of Yellowstone*

A TEAM OF EXPLORERS in the American "Wild West" of 1871 was suddenly stopped short early one morning by "a magnificent parting display." Ten thousand gallons of superhot water shot "100 to 150 feet" into the air. This happened with little or no warning, the group's leader, Ferdinand V. Hayden, reported. He watched in awe as "a succession of impulses" held "the column of water steadily for the space of fifteen minutes."

Leap forward more than 120 years into Yellowstone National Park and think of the millions of visitors from all over the world who have come to see and photograph that same column of water.

Today, they are not surprised to see the geyser, which was named Old Faithful because it never fails to erupt about once every hour.

Of the millions of photographs taken of Old Faithful, the first published photo, taken during the 1871 expedition, remains the most dramatic, the most famous, and the most important. That photograph of Old Faithful, and other photos of the Yellowstone region, helped to make U.S. history. They played a historic role in the establishment of Yellowstone National Park.

The history-making photographer who took the photos was William Henry Jackson, who had the eye of an artist, the curiosity of an explorer, and the spirit of an adventurer.

By the time Jackson died at age ninety-nine, in 1942, his life had spanned American history from the Civil War to World War II. It was an exciting life.

As he recalled in his autobiography: "I have marched off to fight in a war [the Civil War], bullywhacked [driven a wagon pulled by twelve oxen] over the Plains while the Sioux and the Cheyennes were still busy taking scalps, climbed unmapped peaks in the Rockies, and frozen my back teeth crossing Siberia in the dead of winter."

Looking back, he commented that "if any work that I have done should have value beyond my own lifetime, I believe it will be the happy labors of the decade 1869–1878." The highlight of that decade was the Yellowstone expedition of 1871.

Jackson trekked through the unexplored territory of the Yellowstone Valley, with his eight-by-ten-inch camera plus two hundred pounds of equipment, most of it carried on the back of "a fat little mule" named Hypo.

Jackson went to Yellowstone at the invitation of Hayden, who was the director of the official government surveys of the Western territories. Hayden wanted to record what his expeditions found. And he recognized Jackson as the photographer who could do it.

Jackson was on the scene because he had done what many other fellow Americans had done: He "went west." His own personal trail led from Vermont, where he had worked as a photographer's assistant, to Omaha, Nebraska, where he opened a photo studio.

When Hayden visited the studio, he was impressed by Jackson's photos of Native Americans, the Union Pacific Railroad as it moved westward, and the incredible scenery of the American West. Hayden was a dynamo, a man always on the move. The Native Americans watched his nonstop style and named him Man-Who-Picks-Up-Stones-Running.

True to his style, Hayden came right to the point with Jackson. He said of the photographs: "This is what I need. I wish I could offer you enough to make it worth your while to spend the summer with me."

"What *could* you offer?" Jackson asked quickly.

Hayden answered: "Only a summer of hard work—and the satisfaction I think you would find in contributing your art to science."

With the wholehearted support of his wife, who took over the running of the photo shop, Jackson accepted immediately, and in 1870 joined Hayden's expedition. It lasted three months as they followed the Oregon-Mormon trail, traveled through Wyoming badlands, and trudged to Pike's Peak before ending up in Denver in the cold and snow of an early winter.

Jackson followed Hayden back to Washington and signed up as the official (paid) photographer for the 1871 expedition to explore the "Yellowstone Legend." In the early 1800s few explorers had penetrated this area in what is now Wyoming. Those who had, returned with incredible tales that people found hard to believe.

As late as 1869, two explorers sent an article about the wonders of Yellowstone to *Lippincott's Magazine* in Philadelphia. The editors found the descriptions unbelievable: explosive geysers, bubbling mud pots, volcanic holes that spouted hot gases. The explorers received a short, blunt rejection: "Thank you, but we do not print fiction."

Jackson later recalled that the public interest was "really enormous." He also realized, along with Hayden, that seeing—in photographs—would be believing.

In 1871, Hayden's thirty-five-man expedition to the upper Yellowstone lasted forty days and covered five hundred miles. U.S. cavalrymen escorted the team into Yellowstone as protection. Once in, the explorers depended on packers and hunters and on the mules who carried their supplies. It was, as Jackson noted, "glorious and nearly impenetrable country," a "wonderland."

At every opportunity, he left the main party of explorers and went off in search of scenes to photograph. He took two or three companions, plus a pack mule to carry his equipment.

Photography in the field was hard work. Jackson had to trek, trudge, climb, and clamber to find the right spot for his camera. He then mounted it on a tripod and focused the lens.

But that was only the beginning. He had to prepare a glass plate on which the photographic image would appear. That meant wetting the plate with chemicals and inserting it into the camera for the photograph. After exposing the plate, he hurried back to his portable darkroom (or "dark box") to develop the negative on the plate before the chemicals dried.

Here's how Jackson described picture-taking in the wilderness: "My invariable practice was to keep it [the "dark box"] in the shade, then, after carefully focussing my camera, return to the box, sensitize a [glass] plate, hurry back to the camera while it was still moist, slip the plate into position, and make the exposure. Next step was to return to the dark box and immediately develop the plate. Then I would go through the entire process once more from a new position."

The process—from camera to dark box, from dark box to camera, and then from camera back to dark box—took forty-five minutes for one photograph.

Taking into account what picture-taking in the wilderness required, the photography historian Beaumont Newhall characterized Jackson's output of two thousand negatives between 1869 and 1875 as "staggering."

The photos showed Mammoth Hot Springs, which Jackson described as "those bubbling caldrons of nature." And they captured the awesome beauty of Tower Falls, Grand Canyon of the Yellowstone, the Great Falls, and the Crater of the Grotto Geyser.

Jackson's Yellowstone photographs became popular throughout the country. They were reproduced as wood engravings published by illustrated publications of the time, and in photographic prints that Americans bought to hang on the wall.

Art historian Peter B. Hales pinpoints the reason why the photos made such an impact: Yellowstone was America's "last outpost of truly surprising, legendary material." The photographs proved that the "Yellowstone Legend" was the real thing.

In Jackson's day, his photographs were as dramatic as were the first pictures of the earth from space one hundred years later. Back in the cities of the Eastern Seaboard, stay-at-home Americans had heard tales of the incredible sights of Yellowstone. Now they saw them.

So did members of Congress after a bill was introduced in December 1871 to establish Yellowstone National Park "as a public park or pleasuring ground for the benefit and enjoyment of the people."

In the campaign to build support for the bill, the Jackson photographs played a prominent part. They were featured in special exhibitions in Washington, and prints were distributed to important congressmen.

Jackson's photographs were a dramatic and influential argument. They said, in effect: "Look how incredible Yellowstone is." They were the pictures that went with the words arguing that Yellowstone should be set aside for all Americans rather than turned over to a few settlers for exploitation.

After the bill passed easily through both houses of Congress, the historic moment came March 1, 1872, when President Ulysses S. Grant signed it into law. It created America's, and the world's, first national park.

Each time a crowd of tourists gathers around a grayish mound shaped like a small volcano and waits for the hourly eruption of Old Faithful, they can trace the magic opportunity to that stroke of President Grant's pen.

Each time they aim their cameras at the "column of water" shooting skyward, they are following in the footsteps of William Henry Jackson.

Each time we admire Jackson's photographs as the first of millions of photographs of Old Faithful, the how, when, and where add to the excitement of looking.

The photograph also stands on its own merits. As the water shoots toward the sky with soaring whiteness, its right edge looks straight and solid and the left side fades away into mist.

In the background, the mountain and its barely visible trees provide a horizon line to reassure the onlooker that the earth remains solid.

In the foreground, thin, sticklike human figures are dwarfed by the size and the force of nature. From where they stand, they are giving homage to nature.

Outside the photograph, at the best possible angle, his camera mounted on a tripod, Jackson the explorer-photographer was looking through his lens and making history. As his son wrote about Jackson: "High and far, from canyon rim and mountain top, his camera had looked out on the West."

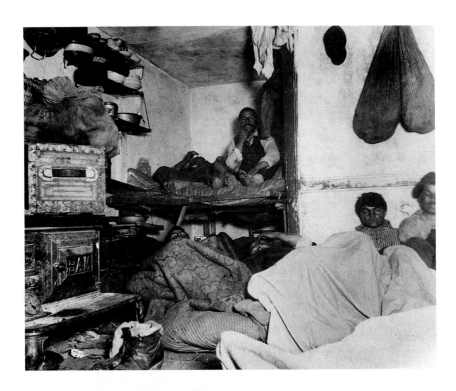

Five Cents a Spot and *Home of an Italian Ragpicker*
(1888–1898) by Jacob Riis. *(The Jacob A. Riis Collection #155
and #157, Museum of the City of New York)*

· 3 ·

"The Power of Fact"

· · ·

Fighting for the Poor with
Pen and Camera

ON A SUNNY DAY in 1888, crusading reporter Jacob Riis set off for
work with an armful of daisies. His three children had picked them
and asked their father to give them to the poor. Stepping off the ferry
in Manhattan, he had gone barely a block when street children began
beseeching him for the blossoms. Soon he was empty-handed.

Arriving at his New York *Tribune* office, Riis demonstrated the
enterprise that made him a genius of social reform. He wrote letters
to several newspapers, asking readers of his column on police news to
bring flowers from their homes to his office for distribution to the poor.

The response was tremendous. Health Department doctors making rounds in the tenements handed out the flowers. Tough-minded
reporters and cynical policemen joined in. One of the largest contrib-
utors was the King's Daughters, a religious good-works society for
women. Soon, Riis asked the group to take over the distribution.

Riis was spurred on to do more for the tenement poor. He decided
to prepare a lecture and to show lantern slides of photographs he had
taken of the slums. An editor of *Scribner's* magazine attended one of

the lectures and suggested an article on tenement life illustrated by Riis's photographs. The article became the book that made him famous in America: *How the Other Half Lives*.

What gave Riis's work such power was the use of photographs. He was the first journalistic crusader to use the camera as a weapon for social change.

He never saw his picture-taking as an art form but as a tool for reform. "The power of fact is the mightiest lever of this or of any day," he wrote in his autobiography.

Riis's crusade for the poor grew out of his background. He had always been close to working people, having worked as a carpenter, miner, laborer, salesman, lumberjack, and trapper, among other jobs. As for newspaper work, it was in his blood. In his native Denmark, which he left in 1870, at the age of twenty-one, Riis had helped his father edit the paper in his hometown of Ribe.

He began his career as a reporter thanks to the principal of a telegraphy school he attended, who wrote a letter of introduction for him to the New York News Association. Riis was hired; this put him in close contact with the neighborhoods of New York: its immigrant slums and financial districts, its factories and cultural institutions.

From the news service he moved to a small weekly in Brooklyn, and finally landed the plum job of police reporter at the New York *Tribune*, where he stayed for ten years, sharpening his muckraking craft with reports on decaying tenements, crime, and the diseases raging among the poor.

Before taking the *Tribune* job, Riis had one of two crucial encounters with technology. Each encounter provided key weapons in his campaign of social reform.

Riis had a stereopticon, a "magic lantern," which could project images with a gaslight like a slide projector. He had bought it thinking it might amuse his children. Then he came up with the idea of using it to project advertisements on street corners at night to earn extra money. He returned to the stereopticon years later to illustrate the lecture attended by the farseeing *Scribner's* editor.

Riis stumbled on a second innovation in a tiny newspaper item in 1887. It described how photographs could be taken in the dark with the use of flash powder. At the time, Riis was frustrated by the fact that words alone couldn't express his outrage at urban misery. He seized the opportunity to use this flash technique to take photographs in the dark tenements and back alleys where he found his stories. With photographs, his facts were documented and dramatized.

As he gathered the photographic evidence of the slum conditions he wanted to change, Riis turned to the lecture hall to spread his message. He traveled across the country with his lantern lectures, hitting the circuit full-time around the turn of the century.

The lectures put Riis in contact with important reformers and clergymen. His book *How the Other Half Lives* was widely discussed in magazines, and ministers quoted from it in their sermons.

Shortly after it was published, future president Teddy Roosevelt left his card on Riis's desk with a note saying he had read the book and wanted to help. Later, Roosevelt called the book "both an enlightenment and an inspiration for which I felt I could never be too grateful."

As Roosevelt rose from president of New York City's police board to New York governor to president of the United States, Riis remained his friend and was his adviser on urban problems. Early in their friendship, Roosevelt closed the notorious police lodging houses— miserable homeless shelters of the day. He also ordered saloons closed on Sunday.

Spurred on by Riis's lectures and writings, the reform movement in New York began tearing down tenements. In 1901, New York State passed the landmark Tenement-House Act, a sweeping law for clearing slums and raising tenement standards. Riis and his "highly human documents" were most responsible for this law, wrote James Ford in *Slums and Housing*, an important early work on the subject.

People's lives improved in other ways thanks to Riis. Desks and playgrounds became mandatory in schools. In an article in the *Evening Sun*, accompanied by six photographs, he exposed contamination in the city's water supply. The story and pictures led to the purchase of the city's Croton watershed. His work helped to pass New York State's Small Park Act of 1887, which created patches of green where slums once reigned.

Summing up Riis's effect on the city where he worked, *The New York Times* wrote in a 1949 editorial marking the hundredth anniversary of his birth that Riis had "startled a complacent New York into a sense of responsibility on slum conditions."

No single Riis photograph changed the lives of the poor. His photographs had a cumulative effect. They were all the more powerful because nothing like them had been seen before, and they were seen everywhere—in newspapers and magazines, in his fourteen books, and at his nationwide lectures.

His flash powder powerfully illuminated the gloomy world of New York's slums, some of the most densely populated areas in the world at the time. The poor, who were usually viewed as a dangerous underclass, suddenly acquired faces. They gained humanity.

The great photographer Ansel Adams called Riis's pictures "magnificent achievements in . . . humanistic photography." Beaumont Newhall, in *History of Photography*, described them as "direct and penetrating, as raw as the sordid scenes which they so often represent."

A good example is the photograph titled "Five Cents a Spot." It appeared in *How the Other Half Lives*, identified as "Unauthorized Lodgings in a Bayard Street Tenement." Riis placed his camera in the doorway of the room, as though the viewer had just opened the door and faced the shock of what was inside.

There is no central focal point. The eye travels from face to face, detail to detail: the black boots next to the stove, the side of a trunk, rows of pots, cloth bags on the wall.

The top bunk is a jumble of arms and legs. The ceiling pushes down on the head of the man seated upright, his hand pensively on his chin. People and objects are squeezed together, reinforcing the idea of crowding that Riis wanted to convey.

Of the scene, Riis wrote: "In a room not thirteen feet either way slept twelve men and women, two or three in bunks set in a sort of alcove, the rest on the floor. A kerosene lamp burned dimly in the fearful atmosphere. . . . Most of the men were lodgers, who slept there for five cents a spot."

The photograph, "Home of an Italian Ragpicker," has an almost religious quality in the tradition of Madonna and child paintings. The desperate-looking mother and child are surrounded by large, impersonal objects: a mattress, a barrel, oversized metal buckets. Riis emphasizes the pair's loneliness by placing the camera low and far back, creating an expanse of wall above and floor in front of them.

Riis used the photograph in one of his early illustrated lectures. He wrote: "See these mothers walking up and down the pavements with their little babes . . . and hear the feeble wails of those little ones! . . . It is only a year ago that the Italian missionary down there wrote to the city mission that he did not know what to do with these Italian children in the hot summer days, for 'no one asked for [cared about] them.' They have been asked for since, thank God!"

The Little Spinner (1908) and *Shrimp Picker* (1911)
by Lewis Hine. (*Courtesy of the Library of Congress*)

· 4 ·

"Bits of Humanity"

Documenting Injustice

THEY ARE SHRIMP PICKERS, cigar rollers, newspaper sellers, bowling-alley pin boys, cotton-field hands, and millworkers. Some look at the camera with an air of bravado mixed with a mischievous grin. Others respond with a tough glare, cigarettes dangling from their mouths. Many, with serious expressions beyond their years, wear oversized adult clothes and ragged shoes.

They are "bits of humanity," some as young as four years old, who peer out of the photographs of Lewis Hine. In fighting against the exploitation of these children, Hine became the best-known reformist photographer of his time, as well as the first great chronicler of the working class.

Whereas Jacob Riis was a journalist who took pictures to shock people into outrage and action, Hine was trained as a sociologist and then set out to document injustice with photographs. He put his camera at the service of causes, becoming a hired gun for social reform. But he was also an artist, whose aesthetic achievement as a photographer is now appreciated.

Hine was born in 1874 in Oshkosh, Wisconsin. The son of a

coffee-shop owner, he worked in an upholstery factory for a time, laboring six days a week, thirteen hours a day. That gave him a taste of the lives of his future subjects. Hine attended the State Normal School in Oshkosh, then the University of Chicago, before studying sociology at Columbia University.

In 1901, when Hine began teaching at the Ethical Cultural School in New York, he acquired a camera and flash gun. He learned to use them through trial and error in order to document life at the school. Soon photography became his passion, and Hine changed careers.

"There were two things I wanted to do," he later explained. "I wanted to show the things that had to be corrected. I wanted to show the things that had to be appreciated."

Over his career, Hine's seventeen photographic projects produced an estimated 40,000 pictures. His first undertaking, which included some of his best-known images, was to record the waves of immigrants arriving at Ellis Island. Hine depicted the immigrants' hopes for a better life and contrasted them with their miserable living conditions. His weapon was a five-by-seven-inch box camera with a rectilinear lens and plunger-activated shutter. He used glass plates, magnesium flash powder, and a wooden tripod.

These pictures, many published in the magazine *Charities and the Commons*, built Hine's reputation among social reformers. Hine was next hired to illustrate *The Pittsburgh Survey*, a portrait of the city in all its aspects. As one of the country's first modern sociological studies, the survey and its powerful pictures of mine and industrial workers were studied around the country.

The project shaped the nation's reform movement by helping to establish working conditions as a public issue. Jane Addams, the famous social worker who founded Hull House in Chicago, said it fed the "veritable zeal for reform" that arose in the years before World War I.

Hine's work for *The Pittsburgh Survey* prepared him for what came next. After the Civil War, many in the South believed the best road to recovery lay in industrialization. Coal was plentiful in Tennessee, Virginia, and Kentucky. The supply of cotton for mills financed by Northern companies was endless. From 1880 to 1904, for example, the number of cotton mills in the South rose from 180 to more than 900.

And labor was cheap, particularly when it was done by children. By the turn of the century, a fourth of millworkers in the South were between the ages of ten and sixteen—more than 40,000 children.

As industry grew and sucked in more child laborers, calls for reform grew too. But reformers had little success in getting state legislatures to pass child-labor laws. In 1904, Edgar Gardner Murphy and Charles J. McElway formed the National Child Labor Committee (NCLC) to lobby for changes.

From the committee's first general meeting came this credo: "It should be plainly said that whatever happens in the sacrifice of adult workers, the public conscience inexorably demands that the children under twelve years of age shall not be touched; that childhood shall be sacred; that industrialism and commercialism shall not be allowed beyond this point to degrade humanity."

The NCLC used articles, pamphlets, lectures, and books to promote its campaign throughout the country. By one estimate, it produced nearly two million pages of material in its first year. It soon turned to photographs to accompany the words. Hine was hired to provide them.

The committee was the first major organization to turn wholeheartedly to photography as a means of social reform. Nothing like it was seen again until government projects recorded the work of the Farm Security Administration in the 1930s.

Using the same camera setup he employed for his Ellis Island pictures, Hine worked full-time for the NCLC from 1908 to 1918. His 5,000 pictures gave the committee's message eyewitness impact. They were widely published in newspapers and magazines; they appeared on posters and were used in illustrated lectures; they accompanied committee reports, many of them written by Hine. He combined words and pictures much as Riis did.

Hine enhanced the value of his photographs as evidence by carefully recording data about the children they portrayed. He measured their height by his vest buttons; he took notes on their age, health, and habits. In so doing, Hine was also protecting himself: Many opponents accused reformers of faking information.

But the power of the photographs, which shocked many around the nation, was inescapable. Hine described his work this way: "In the early days of my child labor activities I was an investigator with a camera attachment . . . but the emphasis became reversed until the camera stole the whole show."

Skeptics were not Hine's only problem. Most factory owners didn't want him around, so he had to turn to trickery to gain entry. Sometimes he posed as a fire inspector, insurance seller, or postcard salesman. At other times, he arrived early in the morning when the workers were there but the bosses were not.

Hine also faced opposition from politicians, who didn't want to upset local business owners. In addition, poor parents were happy to get the extra income earned by their children. And many middle-class people considered work a worthy, even virtuous, activity for children.

Hine wrote much of the information he gathered on the backs of his pictures. Typical is the following: "View of Gulf Coast cannery at 7:00 a.m. Many tiny workers here, some of whom began to arrive at the factory as early as 5 o'clock, an hour before daylight on a damp foggy day. The whistle had blown and they stood around merely to hold their places. When the 'catch' has been good, they begin work early, but today it was not good so they were waiting for daylight."

Hine traveled tens of thousands of miles for the NCLC. He went to seafood-packing plants in the Gulf Coast states, textile mills in New England, tobacco plants in the South. He saw children working in dangerous coal mines in Pennsylvania. In New York and Washington, he photographed small boys selling newspapers in freezing nighttime temperatures. Beet pickers were his subject in Colorado, glassworks laborers in New Jersey.

Many children didn't attend school, and those who did were too exhausted to pay attention. In Mississippi, cannery workers as young as five years old would begin work at three A.M. Delivery boys in Texas worked in the worst part of town and quickly entered the underworld.

The 1910 census showed that 18.4 percent of U.S. children between the ages of ten and eighteen worked. This was two million children—and the figure does not include children under age ten or those working part-time.

The NCLC campaign for reform went slowly, meeting tough resistance from industry owners around the country. But drawing on the power of Hine's work, the campaign began to have an effect.

By 1914, every state in the country had child-labor laws. Thirty-five states barred workers under age fourteen or workdays longer than eight hours for those under sixteen. Thirty-six states had factory inspectors and other protection.

But many of these state laws lacked bite or weren't enforced. So the NCLC pressured the U.S. Commerce Department to set up the

United States Children's Bureau in 1912. It helped persuade Congress to pass a national child-labor law in 1916, though the Supreme Court found the measure unconstitutional two years later. Another law was passed in 1919; it, too, was overturned.

In 1924, an effort to establish a constitutional amendment limiting child labor failed. Finally, in 1938 national protection of young workers was established, with the Fair Labor Standards Act pushed by President Franklin D. Roosevelt.

It was a painfully slow road to social reform, but all along Hine's photographs pointed the way. The NCLC's chairman, Owen R. Love-joy, credited Hine with an important role in reform: "In my judgment, the work you did under my direction for the National Child Labor Committee was more responsible than any or all other efforts to bring the facts and conditions of child employment to public attention."

The NCLC continues to honor Hine's work by bestowing the Lewis Hine Award for Distinguished Service to Children and Youth. In 1992, the recipient was Hillary Rodham Clinton, wife of President Bill Clinton.

Hine's work was vital for three reasons. His pictures were the best evidence the committee had in its lobbying efforts. They turned child labor into a national issue. And as Riis's photos did for slum dwellers, they turned "child workers" into human beings, who look forlorn, smoke cigarettes, frown, and also manage to smile.

Despite his sociological bent, Hine understood that photographs were more than dry evidence. In composing a picture, he took care to establish a center of interest and to consider the play of light, for example by silhouetting a subject in the light from a window or door.

Hine placed the "Shrimp Picker" in front of a huge mound of oyster shells, emphasizing the boy's smallness and youth. The shrimp picker's expression is serious, showing faint impatience to get on with his work. Your eye travels down to his shoeless feet—and then you realize he must walk barefoot over all these shells.

Here is Hine's caption: "Manuel, the young shrimp-picker, five years old, and a mountain of child-labor oyster shells behind him. He worked last year. Understands not a word of English. Dunbar, Lopez, Dukate Company." The photograph was taken in Biloxi, Mississippi, in February 1911.

"The Little Spinner" is a classic Hine photo, combining a striking visual image with a social message. The ragged little girl looks chained to the machinery in a Carolina cotton mill. The tilt of her head, the position of her arm focus attention on the center of her world—an endless row of spindles.

Rays of sunlight bring the outside world of play and freedom into the shadows of the cramped space where she works. Her situation is echoed by another little girl in the background. The two have nothing to do with each other. They are not playmates. They are slaves to the process of spinning cotton. The machine is their "playmate."

Hine identified the power of such images in his career-long campaign for reform. He said of such a photograph "sympathetically interpreted":

"What a lever we have for the social uplift."

Migrant Mother (1936) by Dorothea Lange.
(Courtesy of the Library of Congress)

· 5 ·

A "Hungry and Desperate Mother"

· · ·

*Capturing the Face of the
Great Depression*

ON A BLEAK, rainy day in March 1936, a solitary photographer was speeding along a California road. She was tired after spending four lonely weeks, taking photographs that showed what the Great Depression of the 1930s had done to Americans in rural California.

Dorothea Lange was in a hurry to get home. In order to arrive by dark, she faced seven straight hours of driving at sixty-five miles an hour. "My eyes were glued to the wet and gleaming highway that stretched out ahead," she later recalled. "I felt freed, for I could lift my mind off my job and think of home."

Out of the corner of her eye, she barely noticed a crude sign with an arrow. It read: PEA-PICKERS CAMP.

She didn't want to stop. She wanted to get home. She kept driving. For twenty miles, she had a debate with herself. One side of her was curious about the camp, wanted to go see it. The other side wanted to keep going. She had already taken plenty of pictures showing the pain and the poverty of migrant farmworkers.

But her curiosity and her passion for capturing life on film got the better of her. "Almost without realizing" what she was doing, she made a U-turn and headed back to the camp. Here's what happened, in her own words:

> I was following instinct, not reason; I drove into that wet and soggy camp and parked my car, like a homing pigeon.
>
> I saw and approached the hungry and desperate mother, as if drawn by a magnet. I do not remember how I explained my presence or my camera to her, but I do remember she asked me no questions. I made five exposures, working closer and closer from the same direction. I did not ask her name or her history. She told me her age, that she was 32. She said that they had been living on frozen vegetables from the surrounding fields, and birds that the children killed. She had just sold the tires from her car to buy food. There she sat in that lean-to tent with her children huddled around her, and seemed to know that my pictures might help her, and so she helped me.

The place was Nipomo, California, and it was filled with pea pickers who had no work because the pea crop was frozen. They were stranded and starving.

Lange looked around and saw them, but she didn't need to take any more photographs. She "knew," she wrote, that in ten minutes of shooting photographs of the mother and children she had captured the full story of the human suffering she was witnessing.

The results were immediate.

Armed with the negatives, Lange told the city editor of the San Francisco *News* about the stranded pea pickers. He contacted the United Press, which got in touch with relief authorities.

On March 10, the *News* published a story under the headline FOOD RUSHED TO STARVING FARM COLONY; the story was accompanied by two of Lange's pictures. An editorial gave her credit: "Ragged, ill, emaciated by hunger, 2,500 men, women and children are rescued after weeks of suffering by the chance visit of a Government photographer to a pea-pickers' camp in San Luis Obispo County. And behind that story lies a moral for California and the Federal Government."

The moral of the story locally was that county and state government should help the migrant workers. Nationally, Lange's photos were part of a larger effort to make Americans sensitive to the suffering in the country's farmlands. The message was that the Great Depression was not a matter of statistics from Washington or reports on a falling stock market.

It was people.

Roy Stryker, an economist, was in charge of recording that message in photographs. The federal government hired him to head the Historical Section of the Resettlement Administration, later called the Farm Security Administration (FSA). The FSA's task was to help farmers; Stryker's task was to "introduce Americans to America."

Stryker sent out photographers to bring back pictures of what was happening to rural Americans and thereby build public support for the government's program to help them. He described his photographers as having one thing in common: "a deep respect for human beings." Between 1935 and 1943, they produced 270,000 photographs. By far the most famous was Lange's photograph, "Migrant Mother."

It became a classic. That single image of the mother with her children clinging to her said it all: This is what the Great Depression did to human beings. This is what it meant when the country's gross national product was cut almost in half between 1929 and 1933, when one out of three Americans in the labor force couldn't find a job.

No other U.S. depression was like this one in its length and in the wholesale poverty and tragedy inflicted upon Americans. The United States didn't fully recover from the Great Depression until the early 1940s when it began spending heavily on defense in preparation for World War II.

Beginning in September 1936, when "Migrant Mother" was published in *Survey Graphic* magazine, the photo appeared everywhere—in magazines, in books, and in exhibitions of photographs. Of all the quarter million photographs taken by Stryker's photographers, this one was requested most of all.

Lange's biographer, Milton Meltzer, reports that she was embarrassed when "the picture was exhibited and published over and over, all around the world, year after year." She insisted on pointing out that she was not "a one-picture photographer."

Nonetheless, that one picture helped to raise America's consciousness about poverty in the country's farmlands. It didn't do this by itself, but it played an important role as photography gave witness. Later, John Steinbeck's 1939 best-seller, *The Grapes of Wrath*, called attention to the suffering of migrant workers; it was made into a 1940 movie. Photography, particularly Lange's work, prepared the way and influenced both the writing of the book and the making of the movie.

The photograph itself has left commentators breathless. When the Museum of Modern Art in New York City held a special exhibition of Lange's photographs in 1966, an essay about "Migrant Mother" in the exhibition catalog called it "inexhaustibly rich . . . a great, perfect, anonymous image." The photograph, it was noted, "leads a life of its own."

Looking at the photograph confirms that it still lives. It is in the tradition of famous mother-and-child images in painting and sculpture. It is about love and determination in the face of suffering and uncertainty.

The face of the mother dominates the photograph. She looks off into the distance with an intense, searching expression. The onlooker sees pain and anxiety along with determination. There is also mystery in her look.

The two children, with their homemade haircuts, cling to their mother, as someone on whom their lives depend. Not seeing their faces, we can only guess what they look like and what their expressions are. This evokes even more feelings, as does the dirty sleeping infant pressed against her.

The mother's right hand, cradling her chin, directs the viewer to her haunting face: her eyes, her furrowed brow, the creases around her mouth, the firm set of her jaw.

If the viewer breaks away from the mother's gaze, the photo's details catch attention: her frayed sleeve, the tilt of each child's head, the ragged, wrinkled look of the clothing.

Thirty-five years after Lange's photograph was taken, Stryker looked back on the photographs taken by his team of photographers and summed up "Migrant Mother." He called it "the ultimate" and said: "It was *the* picture" among all the photographs taken. "The others were marvelous but that was special."

Fifty years later, *The New York Times* described the woman's "careworn, resolute face" as "a symbol of the grinding poverty of the Depression."

As one of the most famous photographs of the twentieth century, "Migrant Mother" shook the conscience of America when it first appeared. And it still does.

Old Glory Goes Up on Mount Suribachi (February 23, 1945) by Joe Rosenthal, Associated Press staff photographer. Awarded 1945 Pulitzer Prize. (*AP/Wide World Photos*)

· 6 ·

Recording "the Soul of a Nation"

· · ·

Touching Off a Wave of
World War II Patriotism

DURING "ONE OF the most viciously fought battles in history," a short, nearsighted war photographer stood on a pile of stones topped by a Japanese sandbag near the top of 548-foot-high Mount Suribachi.

It was about noon on February 23, 1945, the fifth day of the U.S. invasion of the Japanese-held Pacific island of Iwo Jima during World War II.

The photographer, whose eyesight was one-twentieth of normal, aimed his camera at five U.S. Marines and a navy medical corpsman struggling to raise the American flag on top of Suribachi. In 1/400 of a second he had his picture.

As the official history of the U.S. Marines records after depicting Iwo Jima as one of history's most vicious battles, "Joe Rosenthal, then an Associated Press photographer, took the flag-raising picture that was to become the most famous of all war photographs."

It's been called the most widely reproduced and re-created photograph in history. At the time, it dominated the front page of almost every American daily newspaper. A painting of it became the symbol of the seventh war-loan drive, appearing on 3.5 million posters, 15,000 outdoor panels, and 175,000 subway car placards.

It appeared on an issue of three-cent stamps and was re-created in a hundred-ton bronze statue erected in Arlington National Cemetery. It also has been re-created in watercolors, oils, pastel, chalk, matchsticks, sandstone, ice, and even hamburger.

By acclamation, Rosenthal's photograph won the 1945 Pulitzer Prize for photography. John Hohenberg, a historian of the prize, states that the photograph "touched off a wave of patriotic pride in American fighting men rarely matched in American history."

World War II was a time of intense patriotism. For five weeks, between the February 19 invasion of Iwo Jima and Iwo's complete capture on March 26, America focused its patriotic fervor on the tiny island. On that island, which is only five miles long and two miles wide, 6,821 Americans died and almost 20,000 were wounded. Another 20,000 Japanese died on its seven and a half square miles of volcanic rock.

The island's strategic location only 660 miles south of Tokyo was what counted, not its size. The United States wanted the island as a base for air attacks on Japan and as a safe landing place for crippled bombers and fighter planes. The Japanese looked upon the island as the front line in defending their homeland.

"Among the Americans who served on Iwo Jima," stated U.S.

admiral Chester W. Nimitz, "uncommon valor was a common virtue."

Rosenthal was there to photograph the valor twenty-one years after he got his first camera, a Brownie, from a coupon catalog when he was a twelve-year-old Boy Scout.

As a combat photographer he was in the middle of the war in the Pacific, covering invasions and carrier-based bomber missions. He hit the beach at Iwo Jima with the 30,000 marines who invaded the island. He risked his life to take photographs of men risking their lives.

Rosenthal's own recollections of Iwo Jima (written for *Collier's* magazine with W. C. Heinz) describe his experiences beginning with the landing under withering Japanese fire: "No man who survived that beach can tell you how he did it. It was like walking through rain and not getting wet, and there is no way you can explain it."

Japanese fire from Mount Suribachi was particularly devastating, making that hill a prime target for the invading marines. So it was a great feat when the marines captured Suribachi. They wanted to plant the American flag on its peak.

When Rosenthal heard about the flag-raising, naturally he wanted to photograph it. He invited a marine photographer and a marine cameraman to come with him. As members of the military, they could carry guns and provide protection.

As they scrambled up Suribachi, the trio had to stop and take cover half a dozen times as marines tossed grenades into caves where Japanese were still holed up. They also had to sidestep land mines and watch for sniper bullets. Halfway up, four marines coming down said they had raised a flag on top of Suribachi. A marine photographer had taken the photograph.

Rosenthal almost turned back.

But he decided to take his own photograph, not knowing, meanwhile, that the marines wanted to replace what was a small flag they had already raised with a large one. They wanted the flag to be seen all over the island and by the ships offshore. So Rosenthal was on hand when six men raised a flag that measured eight feet by four feet eight inches.

Rosenthal stood inside the rim of an extinct volcano to get his photo. At five feet five inches, he wasn't tall enough to get the picture he wanted. So he piled up stones and put a Japanese sandbag on top of them.

Standing atop his makeshift platform, Rosenthal took three photographs, one of the flag-raising, one of the marines tying down the iron pipe that was the flagpole, and a posed photograph of cheering marines.

It was the flag-raising photo that made history.

"In that moment," said the editors of *U.S. Camera* magazine in giving the photograph a special award, "Rosenthal's camera recorded the soul of a nation." *Life* magazine put the photograph on a par with the painting of Washington crossing the Delaware.

The photograph also reflects the human costs of war: Within a few days, three of the men in the photo were killed in the continuing bloodshed on Iwo Jima.

Of the photograph itself, Rosenthal commented on "the things that happened quite accidentally to give that picture its qualities." He cited the sky, the heaviness of the pipe that became a flagpole, the wind, and the terrain:

"The sky was overcast, but just enough sunlight fell from almost directly overhead, because it happened to be about noon, to give the figures a sculptural depth. The 20-foot pipe was heavy, which meant the men had to strain to get it up, imparting that feeling of action. The wind just whipped the flag out over the heads of the group, and at their feet the disrupted terrain and the broken stalks of the shrubbery exemplified the turbulence of war."

Of the photo's significance, Rosenthal observed: "To get that flag up there, America's fighting men had to die on the island and on other islands and off the shores and in the air. What difference does it make who took the picture? I took it, but the Marines took Iwo Jima."

Truman's Historic Decision—Atomic Bombing of Hiroshima
(August 6, 1945) by Sergeant George R. Caron.
(AP/Wide World Photos)

· 7 ·

"The Most Terrible Weapon Ever Known"

Haunting Humankind
with a Mushroom Cloud

AT 8:15 A.M. on August 6, 1945, Toshinki Sasaki turned to talk to a fellow worker in the personnel department of the East Asia Tin Works.

Dr. Masakuzu Fujii sat down to read the newspaper on the porch of his private hospital.

Mrs. Hatsuyo Nakamura, the widow of a tailor, was watching a neighbor from her kitchen window. He had to tear his house down because it was in the path of fire lanes the government was creating. The lanes were designed to keep fires under control after a bombing attack. She was almost in tears as she watched what he had to do.

At 31,600 feet above them, Captain Robert Lewis, copilot of a B-29 called *Enola Gay*, had put aside the letter he was writing to his mother. As the B-29 approached its target, he wrote that the "final touches" had been put on assembling the single bomb on board:

"We are now loaded. The bomb is alive. It is a funny feeling knowing it is right in back of you. Knock wood. . . . We have set the automatic. We have reached proper altitude. . . . Not long now, folks. . . ."

Sergeant George R. Caron, tail gunner of the *Enola Gay*, was holding an aerial camera, ready to begin photographing when the 9,000-pound bomb, called Little Boy, was dropped on the port of Hiroshima on the northern coast of Japan's Inland Sea.

On board the U.S.S. *Augusta*, the president of the United States, Harry S Truman, was listening to the ship's radio. He was waiting for news on the mission of a single plane carrying a single bomb unlike any weapon in the long, terrible history of war.

World War II was rushing toward its conclusion. The war in Europe had been won with the surrender of Germany on May 7, 1945. The world's attention was focused on the Pacific, where the Allies were closing in on Japan. U.S. forces were capturing central Pacific islands. The islands were bombed from the sea and from the air, and then invaded.

The sky over Japan itself rained death and destruction. From March to July 1945, B-29s dropped 100,000 tons of bombs on sixty-two Japanese cities. On one March night alone, Tokyo was turned into an inferno.

But the Japanese still showed no signs of surrendering, and the one thing that the United States wanted to avoid was an invasion of Japan. It was estimated that the staggering price of such an invasion could be as high as a million U.S. casualties and conceivably ten million to twenty million Japanese.

To bring about a quick surrender and avoid such an invasion,

President Truman made the decision to drop *the* bomb—the atomic bomb—on Japan. He himself had only learned about the bomb in April, after becoming president upon the death of Franklin Delano Roosevelt. Truman's secretary of war, Henry L. Stimson, told him that "the most terrible weapon ever known in human history" was almost ready for use.

From the beginning, Truman realized what a decision to drop *the* bomb meant: "a decision which no man in history has ever had to make." On that morning in August 1945, while the President waited, the 245,000 people of Hiroshima began a day like many other wartime days in their city: an early-morning air-raid warning, then an all clear. The morning was still, cool, and pleasant.

Then something fell upon Hiroshima that changed the world forever.

Enola Gay dropped Little Boy. The bomb was attached to parachutes. Built-in devices exploded the bomb 2,000 feet above central Hiroshima.

An awesome flash of light cut across the sky. The explosion generated heat that reached one million degrees Fahrenheit on the ground. It picked up houses and threw them across the street. It picked up an entire hospital, cinema, and hotel and flung them into the river. Fires broke out instantly over an area within two miles of "ground zero."

Of the 76,000 buildings in the city, 70,000 were damaged or destroyed. The Japanese later identified 78,000 Japanese who were killed instantly or soon thereafter. Another 37,000 simply disappeared. The vast majority were civilian men, women, and children.

Author John Hersey, who wrote the first detailed account of what happened to Hiroshima, focused on six survivors. They included the clerk, the doctor, and the tailor's widow who were going about their daily lives when the bomb fell. Hersey concluded: "It would be impossible to say what horrors were embedded in the minds of the children who lived through the day of the bombing in Hiroshima."

The city was transformed into a gruesome nightmare of rubble, dust, destruction, dead bodies, and horribly mutilated men, women, and children. Fifteen minutes after the blast, a thick, choking cloud of dust made it look as if the sun had set over Hiroshima.

High in the sky, the *Enola Gay*, which was climbing steeply at maximum speed, was jolted by shock waves. A fireball shot upward, surrounded by purple clouds. Within three minutes, a mushroom-shaped cloud reached 30,000 feet.

In the tail of the B-29, Sergeant Caron clicked away with his aerial camera, capturing images of what *Life* magazine described as "a great mushrooming cloud of dust and smoke."

Three days later, another atomic bomb was dropped over Nagasaki, one of Japan's largest shipbuilding and ship-repair centers. *New York Times* reporter William Laurence was on hand to describe the explosion. He saw "a giant ball of fire rise as though from the bowels of the earth, belching forth enormous white smoke rings." Next, there was "a giant pillar of purple fire, ten thousand feet high, shooting skyward with enormous speed. . . .

"Then . . . there came shooting out of the top a giant mushroom that increased the height of the pillar to a total of 45,000 feet. The mushroom top was even more alive than the pillar, seething and boiling."

On the day after the Nagasaki attack, Japan, reeling under the impact of the two atomic attacks, offered to surrender. Negotiations went back and forth. Then, at midday on August 15, Emperor Hirohito broadcast Japan's surrender to a world worn out by World War II.

Life magazine summed up the reaction in its August 20, 1945, issue: "The people of the world, although thrilled by the prospect of peace, were shaken by the new weapon, which had brought it about."

The same issue of *Life* published large pictures of the mushroom clouds over Hiroshima and Nagasaki. The pictures derived their impact and their meaning from the event itself, which changed the meaning of all-out war. The message was frightening: Humankind now had the power to destroy itself.

The photograph of the mushroom cloud became the way Americans, as well as the rest of the world's people, "see" the weapon that can destroy us. It is a direct, simple visual statement about standing at the edge of an abyss. It is the single image that represents nuclear war. In black and white, in a cloud formation that tears apart the sky, the photograph sends its message.

Sergeant Caron's photograph not only marks the event. It puts a frightening face on a message that no American, nor anyone else in the world, could ignore:

A mushroom cloud created by humankind hangs over earth, powerful enough to extinguish the life force of the planet.

Index

DATE

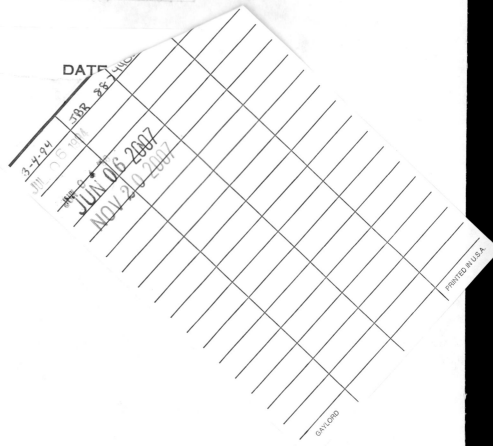

3-4-94

JUL 06 1994

JUN 06 2007

NOV 20 2007

GAYLORD   PRINTED IN U.S.A.